Dish Machine Temperature and Chemical Log

by Joshua R. Embry | www.embryinc.com

Different dish machines have different sanitizing properties and processes, a space is left below for you to define your operating temperature range as well as define the type of chemical requirements your specific machine has. This is vital to ensuring your employees are measuring and recording information based on your standards. This booklet contains forms for 5 years of data measurements.

Machine Name/Model:______________________________

Temperature Range: ________________________________

Chemical Measurement:_____________________________

Process Owner:__________________________________

The following pages contain 5 years worth of temperature and chemical logs for checking your machine 3 times per day. This should be done prior to each meal rush to ensure that your machine is correctly sanitizing dishes and preventing the spread of disease of food borne illness.

Month/Year ________________

Date/Initials	Morn. Temp	Morn. Chems	Lunch Temp	Lunch Chems	Dinner Temp	Dinner Chems
Ex. 3/2/2025 JRE	215F	Okay	211F	Okay	219F	Okay

Month/Year ________________

Date/Initials	Morn. Temp	Morn. Chems	Lunch Temp	Lunch Chems	Dinner Temp	Dinner Chems
Ex. 3/2/2025 JRE	215F	Okay	211F	Okay	219F	Okay

Month/Year ________________

Date/Initials	Morn. Temp	Morn. Chems	Lunch Temp	Lunch Chems	Dinner Temp	Dinner Chems
Ex. 3/2/2025 JRE	215F	Okay	211F	Okay	219F	Okay

Month/Year ________________

Date/Initials	**Morn. Temp**	**Morn. Chems**	**Lunch Temp**	**Lunch Chems**	**Dinner Temp**	**Dinner Chems**
Ex. 3/2/2025 JRE	215F	Okay	211F	Okay	219F	Okay

Month/Year ________________

Date/Initials	Morn. Temp	Morn. Chems	Lunch Temp	Lunch Chems	Dinner Temp	Dinner Chems
Ex. 3/2/2025 JRE	215F	Okay	211F	Okay	219F	Okay

Month/Year ________________

Date/Initials	Morn. Temp	Morn. Chems	Lunch Temp	Lunch Chems	Dinner Temp	Dinner Chems
Ex. 3/2/2025 JRE	215F	Okay	211F	Okay	219F	Okay

Month/Year ________________

Date/Initials	Morn. Temp	Morn. Chems	Lunch Temp	Lunch Chems	Dinner Temp	Dinner Chems
Ex. 3/2/2025 JRE	215F	Okay	211F	Okay	219F	Okay

Month/Year _______________

Date/Initials	Morn. Temp	Morn. Chems	Lunch Temp	Lunch Chems	Dinner Temp	Dinner Chems
Ex. 3/2/2025 JRE	215F	Okay	211F	Okay	219F	Okay

Month/Year ________________

Date/Initials	Morn. Temp	Morn. Chems	Lunch Temp	Lunch Chems	Dinner Temp	Dinner Chems
Ex. 3/2/2025 JRE	215F	Okay	211F	Okay	219F	Okay

Month/Year ________________

Date/Initials	Morn. Temp	Morn. Chems	Lunch Temp	Lunch Chems	Dinner Temp	Dinner Chems
Ex. 3/2/2025 JRE	215F	Okay	211F	Okay	219F	Okay

Month/Year ________________

Date/Initials	Morn. Temp	Morn. Chems	Lunch Temp	Lunch Chems	Dinner Temp	Dinner Chems
Ex. 3/2/2025 JRE	215F	Okay	211F	Okay	219F	Okay

Month/Year ______________

Date/Initials	Morn. Temp	Morn. Chems	Lunch Temp	Lunch Chems	Dinner Temp	Dinner Chems
Ex. 3/2/2025 JRE	215F	Okay	211F	Okay	219F	Okay

Month/Year ________________

Date/Initials	Morn. Temp	Morn. Chems	Lunch Temp	Lunch Chems	Dinner Temp	Dinner Chems
Ex. 3/2/2025 JRE	215F	Okay	211F	Okay	219F	Okay

Month/Year ________________

Date/Initials	Morn. Temp	Morn. Chems	Lunch Temp	Lunch Chems	Dinner Temp	Dinner Chems
Ex. 3/2/2025 JRE	215F	Okay	211F	Okay	219F	Okay

Month/Year ________________

Date/Initials	**Morn. Temp**	**Morn. Chems**	**Lunch Temp**	**Lunch Chems**	**Dinner Temp**	**Dinner Chems**
Ex. 3/2/2025 JRE	215F	Okay	211F	Okay	219F	Okay

Month/Year ________________

Date/Initials	Morn. Temp	Morn. Chems	Lunch Temp	Lunch Chems	Dinner Temp	Dinner Chems
Ex. 3/2/2025 JRE	215F	Okay	211F	Okay	219F	Okay

Month/Year ________________

Date/Initials	Morn. Temp	Morn. Chems	Lunch Temp	Lunch Chems	Dinner Temp	Dinner Chems
Ex. 3/2/2025 JRE	215F	Okay	211F	Okay	219F	Okay

Month/Year ________________

Date/Initials	Morn. Temp	Morn. Chems	Lunch Temp	Lunch Chems	Dinner Temp	Dinner Chems
Ex. 3/2/2025 JRE	215F	Okay	211F	Okay	219F	Okay

Month/Year ________________

Date/Initials	Morn. Temp	Morn. Chems	Lunch Temp	Lunch Chems	Dinner Temp	Dinner Chems
Ex. 3/2/2025 JRE	215F	Okay	211F	Okay	219F	Okay

Month/Year ________________

Date/Initials	Morn. Temp	Morn. Chems	Lunch Temp	Lunch Chems	Dinner Temp	Dinner Chems
Ex. 3/2/2025 JRE	215F	Okay	211F	Okay	219F	Okay

Month/Year ________________

Date/Initials	Morn. Temp	Morn. Chems	Lunch Temp	Lunch Chems	Dinner Temp	Dinner Chems
Ex. 3/2/2025 JRE	215F	Okay	211F	Okay	219F	Okay

Month/Year ________________

Date/Initials	Morn. Temp	Morn. Chems	Lunch Temp	Lunch Chems	Dinner Temp	Dinner Chems
Ex. 3/2/2025 JRE	215F	Okay	211F	Okay	219F	Okay

Month/Year ________________

Date/Initials	Morn. Temp	Morn. Chems	Lunch Temp	Lunch Chems	Dinner Temp	Dinner Chems
Ex. 3/2/2025 JRE	215F	Okay	211F	Okay	219F	Okay

Month/Year ________________

Date/Initials	Morn. Temp	Morn. Chems	Lunch Temp	Lunch Chems	Dinner Temp	Dinner Chems
Ex. 3/2/2025 JRE	215F	Okay	211F	Okay	219F	Okay

Month/Year ________________

Date/Initials	Morn. Temp	Morn. Chems	Lunch Temp	Lunch Chems	Dinner Temp	Dinner Chems
Ex. 3/2/2025 JRE	215F	Okay	211F	Okay	219F	Okay

Month/Year ________________

Date/Initials	Morn. Temp	Morn. Chems	Lunch Temp	Lunch Chems	Dinner Temp	Dinner Chems
Ex. 3/2/2025 JRE	215F	Okay	211F	Okay	219F	Okay

Month/Year ________________

Date/Initials	Morn. Temp	Morn. Chems	Lunch Temp	Lunch Chems	Dinner Temp	Dinner Chems
Ex. 3/2/2025 JRE	215F	Okay	211F	Okay	219F	Okay

Month/Year ________________

Date/Initials	Morn. Temp	Morn. Chems	Lunch Temp	Lunch Chems	Dinner Temp	Dinner Chems
Ex. 3/2/2025 JRE	215F	Okay	211F	Okay	219F	Okay

Month/Year ________________

Date/Initials	Morn. Temp	Morn. Chems	Lunch Temp	Lunch Chems	Dinner Temp	Dinner Chems
Ex. 3/2/2025 JRE	215F	Okay	211F	Okay	219F	Okay

Month/Year ________________

Date/Initials	Morn. Temp	Morn. Chems	Lunch Temp	Lunch Chems	Dinner Temp	Dinner Chems
Ex. 3/2/2025 JRE	215F	Okay	211F	Okay	219F	Okay

Month/Year ________________

Date/Initials	Morn. Temp	Morn. Chems	Lunch Temp	Lunch Chems	Dinner Temp	Dinner Chems
Ex. 3/2/2025 JRE	215F	Okay	211F	Okay	219F	Okay

Month/Year ________________

Date/Initials	Morn. Temp	Morn. Chems	Lunch Temp	Lunch Chems	Dinner Temp	Dinner Chems
Ex. 3/2/2025 JRE	215F	Okay	211F	Okay	219F	Okay

Month/Year ________________

Date/Initials	Morn. Temp	Morn. Chems	Lunch Temp	Lunch Chems	Dinner Temp	Dinner Chems
Ex. 3/2/2025 JRE	215F	Okay	211F	Okay	219F	Okay

Month/Year ________________

Date/Initials	Morn. Temp	Morn. Chems	Lunch Temp	Lunch Chems	Dinner Temp	Dinner Chems
Ex. 3/2/2025 JRE	215F	Okay	211F	Okay	219F	Okay

Month/Year ________________

Date/Initials	Morn. Temp	Morn. Chems	Lunch Temp	Lunch Chems	Dinner Temp	Dinner Chems
Ex. 3/2/2025 JRE	215F	Okay	211F	Okay	219F	Okay

Month/Year ________________

Date/Initials	Morn. Temp	Morn. Chems	Lunch Temp	Lunch Chems	Dinner Temp	Dinner Chems
Ex. 3/2/2025 JRE	215F	Okay	211F	Okay	219F	Okay

Month/Year ________________

Date/Initials	Morn. Temp	Morn. Chems	Lunch Temp	Lunch Chems	Dinner Temp	Dinner Chems
Ex. 3/2/2025 JRE	215F	Okay	211F	Okay	219F	Okay

Month/Year ________________

Date/Initials	Morn. Temp	Morn. Chems	Lunch Temp	Lunch Chems	Dinner Temp	Dinner Chems
Ex. 3/2/2025 JRE	215F	Okay	211F	Okay	219F	Okay

Month/Year ________________

Date/Initials	Morn. Temp	Morn. Chems	Lunch Temp	Lunch Chems	Dinner Temp	Dinner Chems
Ex. 3/2/2025 JRE	215F	Okay	211F	Okay	219F	Okay

Month/Year ________________

Date/Initials	Morn. Temp	Morn. Chems	Lunch Temp	Lunch Chems	Dinner Temp	Dinner Chems
Ex. 3/2/2025 JRE	215F	Okay	211F	Okay	219F	Okay

Month/Year ________________

Date/Initials	Morn. Temp	Morn. Chems	Lunch Temp	Lunch Chems	Dinner Temp	Dinner Chems
Ex. 3/2/2025 JRE	215F	Okay	211F	Okay	219F	Okay

Month/Year ________________

Date/Initials	Morn. Temp	Morn. Chems	Lunch Temp	Lunch Chems	Dinner Temp	Dinner Chems
Ex. 3/2/2025 JRE	215F	Okay	211F	Okay	219F	Okay

Month/Year __________________

Date/Initials	Morn. Temp	Morn. Chems	Lunch Temp	Lunch Chems	Dinner Temp	Dinner Chems
Ex. 3/2/2025 JRE	215F	Okay	211F	Okay	219F	Okay

Month/Year ______________

Date/Initials	Morn. Temp	Morn. Chems	Lunch Temp	Lunch Chems	Dinner Temp	Dinner Chems
Ex. 3/2/2025 JRE	215F	Okay	211F	Okay	219F	Okay

Month/Year ________________

Date/Initials	Morn. Temp	Morn. Chems	Lunch Temp	Lunch Chems	Dinner Temp	Dinner Chems
Ex. 3/2/2025 JRE	215F	Okay	211F	Okay	219F	Okay

Month/Year ________________

Date/Initials	Morn. Temp	Morn. Chems	Lunch Temp	Lunch Chems	Dinner Temp	Dinner Chems
Ex. 3/2/2025 JRE	215F	Okay	211F	Okay	219F	Okay

Month/Year ________________

Date/Initials	Morn. Temp	Morn. Chems	Lunch Temp	Lunch Chems	Dinner Temp	Dinner Chems
Ex. 3/2/2025 JRE	215F	Okay	211F	Okay	219F	Okay

Month/Year ________________

Date/Initials	Morn. Temp	Morn. Chems	Lunch Temp	Lunch Chems	Dinner Temp	Dinner Chems
Ex. 3/2/2025 JRE	215F	Okay	211F	Okay	219F	Okay

Month/Year ________________

Date/Initials	Morn. Temp	Morn. Chems	Lunch Temp	Lunch Chems	Dinner Temp	Dinner Chems
Ex. 3/2/2025 JRE	215F	Okay	211F	Okay	219F	Okay

Month/Year ________________

Date/Initials	Morn. Temp	Morn. Chems	Lunch Temp	Lunch Chems	Dinner Temp	Dinner Chems
Ex. 3/2/2025 JRE	215F	Okay	211F	Okay	219F	Okay

Month/Year ________________

Date/Initials	Morn. Temp	Morn. Chems	Lunch Temp	Lunch Chems	Dinner Temp	Dinner Chems
Ex. 3/2/2025 JRE	215F	Okay	211F	Okay	219F	Okay

Month/Year ________________

Date/Initials	Morn. Temp	Morn. Chems	Lunch Temp	Lunch Chems	Dinner Temp	Dinner Chems
Ex. 3/2/2025 JRE	215F	Okay	211F	Okay	219F	Okay

Month/Year ________________

Date/Initials	Morn. Temp	Morn. Chems	Lunch Temp	Lunch Chems	Dinner Temp	Dinner Chems
Ex. 3/2/2025 JRE	215F	Okay	211F	Okay	219F	Okay

Month/Year ________________

Date/Initials	Morn. Temp	Morn. Chems	Lunch Temp	Lunch Chems	Dinner Temp	Dinner Chems
Ex. 3/2/2025 JRE	215F	Okay	211F	Okay	219F	Okay

Month/Year ________________

Date/Initials	Morn. Temp	Morn. Chems	Lunch Temp	Lunch Chems	Dinner Temp	Dinner Chems
Ex. 3/2/2025 JRE	215F	Okay	211F	Okay	219F	Okay

Month/Year ________________

Date/Initials	Morn. Temp	Morn. Chems	Lunch Temp	Lunch Chems	Dinner Temp	Dinner Chems
Ex. 3/2/2025 JRE	215F	Okay	211F	Okay	219F	Okay

Month/Year ________________

Date/Initials	Morn. Temp	Morn. Chems	Lunch Temp	Lunch Chems	Dinner Temp	Dinner Chems
Ex. 3/2/2025 JRE	215F	Okay	211F	Okay	219F	Okay

Month/Year ________________

Date/Initials	Morn. Temp	Morn. Chems	Lunch Temp	Lunch Chems	Dinner Temp	Dinner Chems
Ex. 3/2/2025 JRE	215F	Okay	211F	Okay	219F	Okay

Month/Year ________________

Date/Initials	Morn. Temp	Morn. Chems	Lunch Temp	Lunch Chems	Dinner Temp	Dinner Chems
Ex. 3/2/2025 JRE	215F	Okay	211F	Okay	219F	Okay

Month/Year ________________

Date/Initials	Morn. Temp	Morn. Chems	Lunch Temp	Lunch Chems	Dinner Temp	Dinner Chems
Ex. 3/2/2025 JRE	215F	Okay	211F	Okay	219F	Okay

Time to reorder

at

www.embryinc.com

www.ingramcontent.com/pod-product-compliance
Lightning Source LLC
Chambersburg PA
CBHW070359190526
45169CB00003B/1048
9781533021779